in her own words

madonna

Mick St. Michael

Omnibus Press

LONDON · NEW YORK · SYDNEY

Copyright © 1990 Omnibus Press
(A Division of Book Sales Limited)

Edited by Chris Charlesworth
Format designed by Ranch Associates
Art Direction by Mike Bell
Cover designed by Lisa Pettibone
Book designed by Evelina Frescura
Artwork by Luke Wakeman
Picture research by Paul Giblin

ISBN 0.7119.2139.3
Order No. OP45814

Exclusive distributors:
Book Sales Limited,
8/9 Frith Street,
London W1V 5TZ, UK.
Music Sales Corporation,
225 Park Avenue South,
New York, NY 10003, USA.
Music Sales Pty Limited,
120 Rothschild Avenue,
Rosebery, NSW 2018, Australia.
To the Music Trade only:
Music Sales Limited,
8/9 Frith Street,
London W1V 5TZ, UK.

Picture credits:

All photographs supplied by London Features International, Pictorial Press, Retna and Starfile.

Every effort has been made to trace the copyright holders of the photographs in this book but one or
two were unreachable. We would be grateful if the photographers concerned would contact us.

Typeset by Capital Setters, London

Printed in Tiptree, Essex by Courier International Limited

CONTENTS

intro

In 1983, the pop world sat up and took notice of a new star. Born Madonna Louise Ciccone in Detroit 25 years earlier, she preferred to be known only by her first name – a move that said much for her self-confidence. There was then and still is only one Madonna. But there are plenty of imitations . . . the Kylies, Sonias, Debbies and many more lesser-known 'Wannabes' to whom Madonna was an inspiration and role model.

Her style was from the street, yet it took her to the top of the charts. Her movies packed out cinemas, her marriage to Brat Packer Sean Penn made front pages everywhere and her music – both on record and in concert – found a ready audience anywhere on earth where you could find a transistor or a disco. In a decade singly lacking in lustre, Madonna's star shone brightest . . . and everywhere people flocked to follow it.

This book majors on Madonna's self-proclaimed views on men, music and pretty much everything in between. Her seven-year career in the public eye has brought much wit and wisdom, the cream of which is encapsulated under a number of convenient chapter headings . . . some of which may surprise you! Nor has Madonna restricted herself to the pop world; her background and rise to fame make equally fascinating reading, vital to understanding what she's become.

Many of Madonna's quotes are provocative – something she consciously developed as a vital part of her strategy of self-publicity. But how much of the real Madonna is revealed here and how much is pure hype? Is Madonna really in search of some great spiritual truth? Or is she just the material girl she sings about? Reading the pick of her pronouncements is the only way to judge.

It's also most instructive (not to mention amusing) to find out what the rest of the entertainment world and society in general has said about her – much of this, it must be said, in the face of some shrewd provocation from Ms Ciccone herself. Did The Cure's mild-mannered Robert Smith really say, "She stinks?" And who, exactly, called her, "A porn queen on heat?" Read on and all will be revealed . . . sorry, those Penthouse pictures are another story!

With her profound influence on pop, fashion and youth culture in general, Madonna was a seminal figure of the eighties who clearly has much to contribute to the nineties. This book is as good an observation post as any from which to assess her past, present and likely future, with one telling advantage . . . the signposts are her own words.

Mick St Michael

Special thanks to Jane Donaldson for her invaluable assistance.

growing up

"My father was very strict and a disciplinarian — we had to go to church every morning before we went to school. When we got home we'd get changed, do our chores, do our homework and eat supper. I wasn't even allowed to watch television until late in my teens. My father didn't like us having idle time on our hands.

"If we didn't have homework he'd find us something to do around the house – he was very adamant about us being productive. My father came from a very poor family, his parents were Italian immigrants."

"He was the youngest of six boys and was the only one who got a college education so it was very important to him that we made the best of our educational opportunities. I turned down a scholarship to the University of Michigan and when I told him I didn't want to go to college but wanted to go to New York and be a dancer it didn't make any sense to him. To him dancing was a hobby and not something you could make a living from."

"When I was tiny my grandmother used to beg me not to go with boys, to love Jesus and be a good girl. I grew up with two images of women: the Virgin and the whore."

"At family reunions I'd climb on a table and start dancing. If I didn't get people's attention that way I'd make some noise."

"I felt really lonely and forlorn, even though my brothers and sisters were in the room with me. My mother had a beautiful red silky nightgown and I remember rubbing against it and going to sleep."

"My mother tried to keep her fear deep inside her and not let us know. Once she was sitting on the couch and I climbed on her back and said, 'Play with me,' and she wouldn't. She couldn't. I got really angry with her and started pounding her with my fist and saying, 'Why are you doing this?' Then I realised she was crying."

"My father was a first generation Italian. My grandparents weren't very educated and I think in a way they represented an old lifestyle that my father really didn't want to have anything to do with. He got an engineering degree and wanted us to have a better life than we did."

"I've inherited some of my father's qualities – stubbornness and being a killjoy. If I go out with friends I'm usually the first one who wants to go home in spite of their protests. When we went to visit relatives my father would always want to go home instead of spending the night with them. That's my father in me."

"From when I was very young I just knew that being a girl and being charming in a feminine sort of way could get me a lot of things, and I milked it for everything I could."

"The thing is, if my father hadn't been strict I wouldn't be who I am today. I think . . . I think that his strictness taught me a certain amount of discipline that has helped me in my life and my career and also made me work harder for things, whether for acceptance or the privilege to do things."

"I left home at 17 and didn't go home that often. It's taken a few years to get close to my family again. There was a time when we weren't talking a lot. It wasn't a case of my just having to go away and make my own way in life. I just didn't feel that he'd truly understand or appreciate it until later . . . Now I'm an established artist I think my father understands what I am trying to do."

"Madonna is my mother's name, she died when I was very young and I loved her a lot so that alone means a lot to me. She was sweet, beautiful and a hard worker. Sometimes I think about how like her I might be but I'll never know – I tend to romanticise and

fantasise about it all the same. It's very rare for an Italian Catholic mother to name her daughter after her – especially as it's such a rare name – so I think maybe it was meant to happen that she died when I was so young. But somehow her spirit is inside of me . . . I don't know whether she can hear me but I tell her things that a girl can only say to her mother. Private things."

"One of the hardest things I've faced in my life was the death of my mother and that's something I really haven't gotten over to this day."

"That period when I knew that my mother wasn't fulfilling her role – and realising that I was losing her – has a lot to do with my fuel, so to speak, my fuel for life. It left me with an intense longing to fill a sort of emptiness."

"It was hard to accept (my stepmother) as an authority figure and the new number one female in my father's life."

"As the oldest girl in my family, I feel like all my adolescence was spent taking care of babies. I think that's when I really thought about how I wanted to get away from all that. I saw myself as the quintessential Cinderella."

"When you're from a big family everybody's really competitive with each other, so aside from just screaming really loud and doing things that got me attention like . . . we would all get in various kinds of trouble to get my father's attention and then be punished accordingly.

"I was really competitive in school with my grades and stuff because my father used to give us rewards if we got 'A's on our report cards. It wasn't so much that I was interested in learning . . . my father gave us 25 cents (about 17 pence in real money) for every 'A' that we got so I wanted to earn the most amount of money."

"When I was a little girl, I wished I was black. All my girlfriends were black. I was living in Pontiac, Michigan, and I was definitely the minority in the neighbourhood. White people were scarce there. All my friends were black and all the music I listened to was black. I was incredibly jealous of all my black girlfriends because

they could have braids in their hair that stuck up everywhere. So I
would go through this incredible ordeal of putting wire in my hair
and braiding it so I could make my hair stick up. I used to make
cornrows and everything. But if being black is synonymous with
having soul, then yes, I feel that I am."

"We lived in a real integrated neighbourhood. We were one of the
only white families, and all the kids had Motown and black stuff.
And they had yard dances in their backyards, little 45 turntables
and a stack of records, and everyone just danced in the driveway
and back yard . . . I really liked The Shirelles, The Ronettes,
Martha Reeves And The Vandellas and The Supremes – they're
the quintessential pop songs."

"I wanted to do everything everybody told me I couldn't do . . .
I couldn't wear make-up, I couldn't wear nylons, I couldn't cut
my hair, I couldn't go on dates, I couldn't even go to the movies
with my friends."

"Everyone in the family studied a musical instrument. My father
was really big on that. Somehow I only took about a year of piano
lessons and I convinced my father to let me take dancing lessons
instead, so I escaped the dreariness of piano lessons every day
which I despised. But there was always music in our house, either
records or the radio or someone singing in the bathtub . . . noise.
Lots of noise."

"I actually studied piano for a year but I quit. Actually my teacher
made me quit because I never went to lessons, I used to hide in a
ditch. I convinced my father to let me take dance lessons instead."

"I had a traditional Catholic upbringing, and I saw the privileges
my older brothers had. They got to stay out late, go to concerts,
play in the neighbourhood. I was left out. Then, when I was
dancing, most of the men were homosexuals, so I was left out
again. Somewhere deep down inside of me is a frustrated
little boy."

"(My father and I) get on very well right now. I mean, it's been up and down. You know, my father is not an incredibly verbal man, and that's been my frustration. He doesn't really express himself. And more than anything, I want my father's approval, whether I want to admit it or not. But he's always been very affectionate with me. I have a million different feelings about my father, but mostly I love him to death. What's difficult for my father is the idea that I don't need him. But I do need him."

"To my superiors I seemed like a very good girl. I was very good at getting into those situations where I was the hall monitor and I reported people who weren't behaving. And I used to torture people."

"It (Detroit) is really desolate, a factory town. Since Motown there hasn't been any real cultural scene there. There's a good jazz scene but that's about it."

making it

"I think your parents give you false expectations
of life. All of us grow up with completely misguided
notions about life and they don't change until you
get out into the world. It's like someone telling you
what love or marriage is: you can't know until you're
there and you have to learn the hard way."

"I really learnt to dance on my own. I watched television a lot and I used to try to copy Shirley Temple when I was a little girl. I used to turn on the record player and dance in the basement by myself and give dance lessons to my girlfriends in my five-year-old manner. As I got older I started giving lessons to boys too, and I remember the first guy I gave lessons to, the song was 'Honky Tonk Women' by The Rolling Stones . . . it was really sexy."

"It really annoyed me that most of the dancers I knew had such a simple-minded view of life. They were really closed up. They got up early, took dance classes all day, and then they went to rehearsal and ate healthy food. Then they went home and went to bed early. They did this every day and they didn't know anything about music or art; they just knew nothing and were completely ignorant.

   "Most of the kids that I knew who were in my ballet class and stuff, were little bratty girls who stared at themselves in the mirror all day. I found myself doing the same thing, ultimately, I did that when I was living in Detroit. I started rebelling and wanting to get out."

"All these girls would come to class with black leotards and pink tights and their hair up in buns with little flowers in it. So I cut my hair really short and I'd grease it so it would be sticking up, and I'd rip my tights so there were runs all over them and I'd make a big cut down the middle of my leotard and put safety pins all the way up it. Anything to stand out from them and say, 'I'm not like you, OK. I'm taking dance classes and everything but I'm not stuck here like you.' Eventually I said to myself, 'Well, if you don't like it Madonna, do what you want to do.' That's when I started exploring other territories and quit going to dance class every day."

"I used to finish school early and rush off to dance classes and I guess my ballet teacher became my introduction to glamour and sophistication. He was very Catholic and disciplined. He's the one who really inspired me. He kept saying, 'You're different' and 'You're beautiful.' He never said I'd make a great dancer. He just said 'You're something special'."

"When I was in tenth grade I knew a girl who was a serious ballet dancer. She looked smarter than your average girl in an interesting off-beat way so I attached myself to her and she took me to ballet

classes. I met Christopher Flynn, a tutor who saved me from my high school turmoil. I loved him. He was a mentor and a father, an imaginary lover . . . he encouraged me to go to New York. He was the one who told me I could do it if I wanted to."

"I used to run in late to my dance classes with ripped up leotards held together with safety pins. I loved doing things for the shock effect."

"I wanted to dance in New York, but all the good companies were full. I couldn't wait five years to get a break so I started going to musical theatre auditions. They took me to Paris and introduced me to awful French boys, took me to expensive restaurants and dragged me round to show their friends what they had found in the gutters of New York. I would throw tantrums and they'd give me money to keep me happy. I felt miserable."

"When I left home and was poor I lived on popcorn, that's why I still love it. If I had a dollar to spare I'd buy popcorn, yoghurt and peanuts. Popcorn is cheap and it fills you up."

"I was sacked from (Dunkin' Donuts) for squirting the donut jelly all over the customers."

"When I was a child, I always thought that the world was mine, that it was a stomping ground for me, full of opportunities. I always had this attitude that I was going to go out into the world and do all the things I wanted to do."

"Sometimes I travel through people, but I think that's true of most ambitious people. If the people can't go with me – whether it's a physical or emotional move – I feel sad about that. But that's part of the tragedy of love."

"When I came to New York, it was the first time I'd ever taken a plane, the first time I'd ever gotten into a taxi-cab, the first time for everything. And I came here with 35 dollars in my pocket. It was the bravest thing I'd ever done. My goal was to conquer the city and I feel I have."

"Although I took to New York straight away I was really lonely. I would take whatever I could in a taxi-cab to wherever I was going to next. I'd take a big breath, grit my teeth, blink back my tears and say, 'I'm gonna do it – I have to do it because there's nowhere else for me to go.''

''When my father came to visit (New York), he was mortified. The place was crawling with cockroaches. There were winos in the hallways, and the entire place smelled like stale beer.''

''I loved getting dressed up and going out on the street and walking around. I didn't have the money to take cabs then, so I took subway trains a lot and I loved seeing the unusual effect I had on people, and now I can't really enjoy that privilege any more because I already have all the attention. I feel like when I walk down the street, people don't see me as an interesting person, they see me as Madonna.''

FINDING IT

''I thought, 'Who's the most successful person in the music industry and who's his manager? I want him'.''

''I worked my butt off before I got where I got and literally starved and lived off the street and ate out of garbage cans before any of this happened.''

''I've been working my ass off for seven years. I've worked for everything that I've got and I worked long and hard so when I got it I thought I deserved it. I always knew that it would happen.''

''I always said I wanted to be famous . . . I never said I wanted to be rich.''

''I knew I was different when I was five. My father brought me up to be competitive. I was encouraged to aim for the top rung of the ladder.''

''Eventually I decided I should try and get pro about (dancing). At about 12 or 13 I started going to the schools where they teach tap, jazz, baton twirling and gymnastics. It was just a place to send hyperactive girls, basically. When I was 14 or 15 I started taking ballet every day.''

''I felt like I was camping outside in the wilderness for seven years. I never had any money and I never had any help. Dealing with all that and having to struggle to survive has made me into the bitch that most people think I am.''

"I want to rule the world. Every time I reach a new peak, I see a new one I want to climb. It's like I can't stop. Maybe I should rest and admire the view, but I can't. I've got to keep on pushing. Why? I don't know. I don't know what motivates me. I just know I've got to do it."

"You have to be patient. I'm not."

THE PRICE OF FAME

"Money's not important. I never think I want to make millions and millions of dollars but I don't want to have to worry about it. The more money you have the more problems you have. I went from making no money to making comparatively a lot and all I've had is problems. Life was simpler when I had no money, when I just barely survived."

"I have more bills, my telephone rings more, I look down at the ground when I'm walking, I take people out to dinner more and sometimes I get this scary feeling that I could do anything that I wanted."

"When (the nude pictures) were taken eight years ago they weren't meant for publication in any magazine. They were taken by these guys who took pictures for nude exhibitions. At the time I wasn't well known and wasn't aware that I was setting myself up for a future scandal. For years I modelled for lots of life studies in art schools. I was a dancer at the time. I was in really good shape and slightly underweight so you could see my muscle definition and my skeleton. I was one of their favourite models because I was easy to draw."

"You got paid 10 dollars an hour (for posing nude). It was a dollar fifty at Burger King. I kept saying, 'It's for Art'."

"I did that work to make money and ended up modelling privately in people's houses so I got involved with photographers. I consider the nude a work of art. I don't see pornography in Michelangelo. Obviously I would have preferred they weren't published but I think when people saw them they said, 'What's the big deal?' It's other people's problems if they turn them into something smutty. That was never my intention."

"At first the *Playboy* photos were very hurtful to me, and I wasn't sure how I felt about them. Now I look back at them and I feel silly that I ever got upset, but I did want to keep some things private. It was like when you're a little girl at school and some nun comes and lifts up your dress in front of everybody and you get really embarrassed. It's not really a terrible thing in the end, but you're not ready for it, and it seems so awful and you seem so exposed. Also *Penthouse* did something really nasty: they sent copies of the magazine to Sean."

"When I was in Japan, somebody called up and said my father had died, just to get me on the phone. It's scary. Strangers feel like they know you because you're a public figure. I've had guys I've never seen before come up to me on the street and try to kiss me."

"There have been times when I've thought 'If I'd known it was going to be like this I wouldn't have tried so hard.' If it ever gets too much, or I feel like I'm being over-scrutinised, or I'm not enjoying it any more, then I won't do it."

"America is a really 'life-negative' society. People want to know all the underneath stuff, your dirty laundry which isn't to say all the stuff the press has been getting on me is negative or dirty or whatever, but there's always a hope, for them, that they'll uncover something really scandalous."

"I do get depressed but not about the press. I'd have to be on tablets not to be depressed. It's not so much that people are being anti-Madonna, but the fact that they are dwelling on something negative when they could be doing something positive with their lives."

"The thing that more than anything annoys me about the paparazzi is that they really feel they have put you where you are. They really think that because you're a celebrity you owe them all the pictures they can get. I think it's completely unfair."

"You can't sit around worrying about people disliking you because they're always going to be there. It can't stop you."

"When I laugh out loud in the streets here (in Britain) I'm made to feel as if I'm doing something wrong. You know that sort of young, bold, aggressive quality that the more reserved and sophisticated British people hate. Most times people aren't very nice to me in Britain."

"I get so much bad press. People associate a girl who's successful with being a bimbo or an airhead. Sexy boys never get bad press."

"I have a lot of young girl fans and they'll start squealing on the trains. People come up and say, 'You look just like Madonna,' and I'll go 'Thank you,' or they'll say 'Are you Madonna?' and I'll say 'Yes.' Then they'll say 'No you're not'."

"I could never have imagined that success could be like this. Yes it was a surprise but I can handle it. I can still laugh about it, so I guess I'm alright."

"When Robert de Niro comes into the airport, there aren't 20 photographers who sit on his limousine and won't allow him to leave. I don't think Al Pacino – or Robert – has been hounded the way I've been."

"There are the nutcases. Basically there are two kinds of nut – the sex maniac who wants a piece of my underwear and the moral majority who condemn me to emotional hell."

STAR CHOICES

"Warner Brothers is a hierarchy of old men, and it's a chauvinist environment to be working in because I'm treated like this sexy little girl. I have to prove them wrong, which has meant not only proving myself to my fans but to my record company as well. That is something that happens when you're a girl. It wouldn't happen to Prince or Michael Jackson.

"I had to do everything on my own and it was hard trying to convince people that I was worth a record deal. After that I had the same problem trying to convince the record company that I had more to offer than a one-off girl singer."

"When I first started I think it offended a lot of people to find out I was white, especially black radio programmers in the American South. So many black artists won't get played that they don't want to give airtime to someone who isn't black. It's not like I'm ripping them off. At least I'm sincere. I don't feel guilty about not being black, though I think ultimately I will be able to cross over bigger because I'm not."

"After I put out two 12-inch disco records and they did fairly well, I thought I must have a manager. So I thought 'Who's the most successful person in the music industry? I want Michael Jackson's

manager.' He came out to New York and saw a show I did. I was so nervous because he'd just seen Prince and thought he was terrible. But he liked my show."

"I think the ultimate challenge is to have some kind of style and grace, even though you haven't got money, or standing in society, or formal education. I had a very middle, lower-middle class sort of upbringing, but I identify with people who've had, at some point in their lives to struggle to survive. It adds another colour to your character."

"Do you really think I'm a material girl? I'm not. Take it – I don't need money I need love."

"I suppose when I ever get to the point of not having the desire to know and the hunger to learn more, then I won't continue to act or write songs."

THE COMPETITION

"When (Madonna clones) first started happening, I kind of got pissed off. You know if you create a sound, then you want to have dibs on it. But then I felt flattered. But it is confusing sometimes, because I'll hear a song on the radio for a second and think it's me. It's uncanny sometimes. There's one girl in particular, a girl named Alisha, who's had a couple of songs. And her voice sounds so much like mine when I sing in a higher register. I was shocked. She's definitely one who stunned me. I think a lot of the imitators are black."

men

"He was so beautiful. I wrote his name all over my
sneakers and on the playground – I used to take off
the top part of the uniform and chase him around."
Her first crush, a boy named Ronny Howard in
fifth grade.

EARLY AFFAIRS

"My first boyfriend was when I was, I guess . . . gee, I think 14 or 15. I fell in love with a boy named Russell. He was the only boy who would dance with me at school, because I was really wild at the high school dances and I danced completely insanely and all the guys were afraid to ask me to dance with them because I basically ignored them anyway. But Russell was a wild dancer and he was a couple of years older and he was more sophisticated . . . so he was the one who had the courage really. So he won my heart, because he wasn't afraid of me . . ."

LATER LOVES

"All my boyfriends turned out to be very helpful to my career. That's not the reason why I stayed with them. I loved them all very much. I'm not Alexis from Dynasty."

"All the men I stepped over to get to the top . . . every one would have me back because they all still love me and I love them."

"They're irresponsible and challenge the norm. I try and rehabilitate them, I'm just trying to be the mother I never had."

THE LADY PREFERS

"I dig skin, lips and Latin men."

"Italian men like to dominate. It's something that I have felt at times in my life."

"I guess a lot of my hot-blooded and passionate temperament is Italian. I like dark brooding men with rough tempers. Italian men like to dominate and sometimes I like to cast myself in the submissive role."

"I don't have many women friends. It's because I haven't found many who are worldly wise and intelligent. Then again, I just seem to get on better with boys . . ."

"Is sex dirty? Only when you don't take a bath."

"I've had some painful experiences with men in my life, just as I've had some incredible experiences. Maybe (on 'Like A Prayer') I'm representing more of the former than the latter. I certainly don't hate men. No, no, no. I couldn't live without them."

"Romance should be spontaneous, but in my career I'm totally in control."

"I prefer effeminate looking men and young boys. There are a lot of very sweet Puerto Rican boys where I live, and if it outrages people when we go out together that's fine by me. Fifteen or sixteen-year-old boys are the best and I like smooth men who aren't afraid to show their emotions and cry. I want to caress a nice smooth body, not a hulk."

marriage

"I can't conceive of living happily ever after or
happiness for a long period of time with one person.
I change so much and my needs change also."

OLD FASHIONED VIEWS

"I guess you know when you're in love when you finally decide that you want to make sacrifices for somebody else, and you want to give something up for somebody else, you don't just concentrate on yourself. Like the love that parents have for their children . . ."

"I would love to have a child. Then after I have a child I would decide whether I'd love to have another child. When I see couples and they've just had a baby and it's newborn and fresh and smelling good, and it's completely pure and perfect and all that, I really want to have one for my own. I want it."

"Marriage is a roller coaster."

"The best thing about being single is that there's always someone else. I wouldn't wish being Mr Madonna on anybody."

THE WEDDING
(August 16, 1985)

"I was jumping up and down on my bed, performing one of my morning rituals and all of a sudden (Sean) gets this look in his eye and all of a sudden I knew what he was thinking. I said, 'Whatever you're thinking I'll say yes to.' That was his chance, so he popped it."

"That whole time was almost too much. I didn't think I was going to be married with 13 helicopters flying over my head. It turned into a circus. In the end I was laughing. At first I was outraged and then I was laughing. You couldn't have written it in a movie. No one would have believed it. It was better than anything like that . . . it was just incredible. It was like a Busby Berkeley musical. Or something that someone would stage to generate a lot of publicity for one of their stars."

THE MARRIAGE

"To me our love feels like a huge hand that comes around my whole body. Sometimes it's all furry and warm and sometimes it's all scratchy and it hurts."

"From the time we got married (people) couldn't make up their minds: they wanted me to be pregnant, or they wanted us to get a divorce. That put a lot of strain on our relationship too, after a while. It's been a character building experience, and a test of love to get through it all."

"A lot of times the press would make up the most awful things that we had never done, fights that we never had. Then sometimes we would have a fight, and we'd read about it and it would be almost spooky, like they'd predicted it or they'd bugged our phones or they were listening in our bedroom. It can be very scary if you let it get to you."

"We are a 'Hollywood couple' so people are going to pay a lot of attention to our marriage and whether it's going to work or not. If we have our fights . . . I think that's pretty normal for young people in the first few years of marriage. It's normal for anybody who's married, but when you put all the pressure that we've had on top of that, I think the fact that we're still together is pretty amazing. You know, we're working it out . . . it's easy to give up but not easy for me to give up."

"Sean will fight for privacy. He wants to protect me . . . as inefficient as his methods may be, he sticks with what he believes in."

"I have to admit I do flirt a lot but I guess Sean knows that by now, flirting is part of my make-up. I'll flirt with anybody, from the garbage man to grandmothers."

"I can never speak for Sean. He will always deal with the press in his own way."

"When I was putting together the 'Who's That Girl' tour, it was always in the back of my mind, 'I wonder what Sean will think of this?' He's extremely opinionated and has really high standards, and sometimes pushes me into making decisions I wouldn't otherwise have made. He's critical and supportive. I really respect his opinion. He has great taste and is a very brilliant man."

1987

"I don't like violence. I never condoned hitting anyone, and I never thought that any violence should have taken place. But on the other hand I understand Sean's anger, and believe me I've wanted to hit (the press) many times. I never would, you know, because I realise that it would just make things worse. Besides, I have chances to vent my anger in ways other than confrontation. I like to fight people and kind of manipulate them into feeling like they're not being fought. I'd rather do it that way."

"I think (Sean) really believes it's a waste of energy. It antagonises the press and generates even more publicity and I think he realises that. But once (the press) realised he was a target for that, they really went out of their way to pick on him, to the point where they would walk down the street and say, 'C'mon, c'mon, hit me, hit me.' It's not fair. And they insult me, and they try to get him to react. You just have to have the strength to rise above it all."

"Sean will always deal with the press in his own way. For myself, I have accommodated the press a great deal. I've done numerous press conferences, numerous press interviews. But I'm a lot more outgoing and verbal in that way than Sean is. Also, in the beginning of my career, I invited controversy and press and publicity, and I don't think he did that at all. He was a very serious actor, and he wasn't interested in having a Hollywood star image and didn't do a lot of interviews, and it took him quite by surprise, whereas I had already kind of thrown myself into that world. And therefore we deal with it differently."

THE AFTERMATH

"I think it was just two people who were basically incompatible at the end. They tried very very hard to make their relationship work but in the end there was something inherently incompatible in their natures."
Steve Bray, Madonna's co-writer, on the break-up of her marriage to Sean Penn.

"I felt that no one wanted us to be together. They celebrated our union, and then they wanted us to be apart. There were rumours about us getting a divorce a week after the wedding. We fought that. You have to be really, really strong and immune . . . very sure of yourself."

"Ultimately I have twinges of regret, but I feel more sadness than anything. Feeling regret is really destructive. I have learned a great deal from my marriage, so much. About everything – mostly about myself."

"I'm a very old fashioned girl. Marriage is a great thing when it's right. And I did celebrate it and embrace it, and I wanted the whole world to know that this was the man I loved more than anything. But there's a price to pay for that, which is something I realise now. Ever since I was in high school, when I was madly in love with someone, I was so proud of that person. I wanted the world to know that I loved him. But once you reveal it to the world – and you're in the public eye – you give it up, and it's not your own any more. I began to realise how important it is to hold on to privacy and keeping things to yourself as much as possible. It's like a runaway train afterwards."

music

"Once I felt really confident about my dancing
I went into music. I started writing songs, but when
I had to get out in front of lots of people and actually
perform them, I encountered all the same fears of
awkwardness and uncertainty that I felt when I first
started dancing. Every time I start something new,
my knees tremble, and I want to learn. I'm afraid
and I'm also excited. I'm just like an open book.
I want to get everything into my head that I can, then
get it out."

RANDOM NOTES

"I became an excellent drummer. I was really strong and I'd had all this dance training so I had all this energy. Instead of dancing for eight hours a day, I was practising the drums for four hours a day – I drove everybody mad."

"I've always been into rhythmic music, party music, but Gotham (an early agency) weren't used to that stuff, and although I'd agreed to do rock and roll, my heart was no longer in it. Soul was my main influence and I wanted my sound to be the kind of music I'd always liked. I wanted to approach it from a very simple point of view because I wasn't an incredible musician. I wanted it to be direct. I still loved to dance and all I wanted to do was to make a record that I would want to dance to, and people would want to listen to on the radio."

"When I was studying ballet I listened to classical music all the time because that's what you listen to when you take class. And I got really interested in it, but just lately I started listening to it all over again and I really miss it. The other day my husband was playing Brahms, I never really listened to him that much and I loved it – it was a concerto. I love Mozart and Chopin. They have some real sweet feminine quality about a lot of their music."

"When I was younger I really liked girl singers like Lulu and those kinda innocent angelic faces . . . Marianne Faithful, that kind of stuff."

"Producers more important than artists? That's bullshit. A good song is a good song."

"Art and music can never be too permissive, especially as they're an alternative to the reactionary attitudes of Reagan and the Moral Majority."

"I think people have too many pretentious ideas about (music) . . . what's artistic and what has integrity and what doesn't. They think if it's simple and accessible, then it's commercial and a total compromise. And if it's masked in mystery, not completely understood and slightly unattractive, it has integrity and is artistic. I don't believe that."

"Music is the main vector of celebrity. When it's a success its impact is just as strong as a bullet hitting the target."

"Music is a very personal statement, but I've always liked to have different characters that I project. I feel that I projected a very specific character for 'Like A Virgin' and that whole business and then created a much different character for my third album. The problem is, in the public's mind, you are your image, your musical image, and I think that those characters are only extensions of me."

"Most of my lyrical ideas come from everyday life. Some are more fantasy motivated along the lines of ideal relationships. In general my songs are a bit of both."

"When you are singing a song you are making yourself very vulnerable. It's almost like crying in front of people. Acting is like that too. It's just a different way of doing it."

"The things that inspire me to make music are the things that arouse my curiosity and make me happy in life . . . every day I try to write in a journal, jotting down thoughts or maybe something I read that impressed me . . . Everything inspires me: a great book or movie, an expression in someone's eyes, children or old men walking down the street. You know what I like to do when I go to parties? I like talking to the butlers and the janitors and stuff – they're the funniest, they inspire me."

"I hate it when people do mastermixes of my records. I don't want to hear my songs changed like that."

"I know that I've created a lot of bad feeling with the Moral Majority or Parents And Children. There's this big scandal about banning music with sexually explicit lyrics, but I think ultimately children, more than anybody, sense the realness of somebody and the goodness of somebody."

"In America Warners don't know how to push me . . . whether to push me as a disco artist or new wave because of the way I look. I'd rather just start another category."

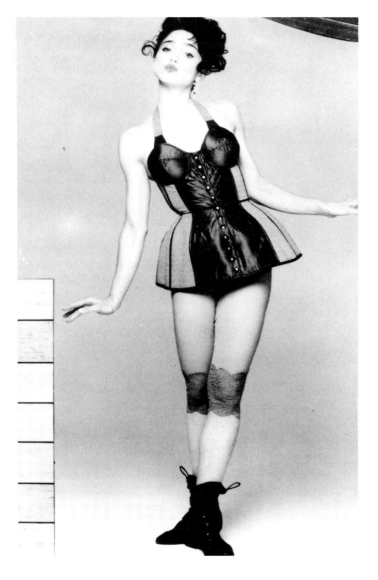

INFLUENCES

"Ella Fitzgerald has an incredible voice. She's the greatest. Joni Mitchell . . . Patsy Cline . . . Chaka Khan – I love her voice. I love all the old soul singers – Marvin Gaye, Frankie Lymon, Sam Cooke. I like really smooth voices like Belafonte and Mathis. My father had all their records. Then there are the gravelly voices – Joe Cocker, Tom Waits and Prince. Prince has an incredible voice."

"I love Ella Fitzgerald more than anything. She has the coolest voice in the world. The way Ella sings scat is unbelievable."

"I can't remember who I saw first, Elton John or David Bowie, but I was punished for seeing both of them because the Arena was a really dangerous part of downtown Detroit and it really wasn't the place for young girls to be going unescorted, which we all were. I think I lied to my father and said I was spending the night at my girlfriend's and then I went off to the concert and both times my father called and found out that I'd gone to the concert. I think I got grounded or something. Like one summer, I wanted to go away to camp or something and I wasn't allowed because I went to see David Bowie. But it was worth it. I borrowed a long black velvet cape from my girlfriend – who knows what I had on underneath it? – and I made a grand entrance. And that was the most important thing."

"Debbie Harry . . . she and Chrissie Hynde were big inspirations to me because they were both women and they were in charge of what they were doing. They were obviously writing their own lyrics and they had very strong images and that gave me courage."

"My favourite music to listen to is baroque, that would be Vivaldi and Bach and Pachelbel."

"One of my all-time favourite poets is Charles Bukowski. I think he's the coolest guy in the world."

"I'm sure that each record I heard influenced me in some way, just like every person you ever meet influences you."

WRITING SONGS WITH OTHERS

"Lots of times Pat Leonard will come up with a piece of music like 'Oh Father' – we did very little to change it musically – he throws the music at me and I just listen to it over and over again. And

somehow the music suggests words to me and I just start writing
words down. Other times I will come to Pat with an idea for a
song, either lyrically or emotionally and say 'Let's do something
like this' or I'll have a melody line in my head which I will sing to
him and he will sort of pound out the chords. It takes a lot longer
to do it that way because I don't play an instrument but ultimately
it's a lot more personal.

"Then with Steve Bray it's the same thing. Sometimes he'll
come up with a track and he'll have a verse and chorus but he
won't have a bridge (between the verse and the chorus) so we'll
write the bridge musically together."

"I like to have control over most of the things in my career but I'm
not a tyrant. I don't have to have it on my album that it's written,
arranged, produced, directed and stars Madonna. To me, to have
total control means you can lose objectivity. What I like is to be
surrounded by really talented, intelligent people you can trust.
And ask them for their advice and get their input. But let's face it.
I'm not going to make an album and not show up for the vocals or
make a video and have nothing to do with the script."

CO-WRITING
WITH PRINCE

"We'd always talked about getting together to write. I went to his
studio in Minnesota and worked on some stuff, just to get an idea
of what it would be like to collaborate. It's a very intimate thing to
write a song together. I've tried with a lot of people and it doesn't
always work."

"We started on a bunch of stuff then we would go on to the next
thing. We just tried to start as many things as we could. We
worked for a few days and then I had to leave to do some other
things and I decided that I didn't want to do a musical with him at
that time."

"It's about the influence of Catholicism in my life and the passion
it provokes in me."

"I've been exploring different kinds of music and discovering
things inside me that I suppose have always been there but I've
never had the confidence and experience to show them before. It's
taken a lot of guts to do this, I've taken more risks with this album
than ever before and I think that growth shows."

"In the past my records tended to be a reflection of current
influences. This album is more about past musical experiences.
The songs 'Keep It Together' and 'Express Yourself', for instance,
are sort of my tributes to Sly And The Family Stone. 'Oh Father'
is my tribute to Simon And Garfunkel, whom I loved. Also the
overall emotional content of the album is drawn from what I was
going through when I was growing up – and I'm still
growing up."

"As it turned out we did it in a very funny way. We sent tapes to
each other back and forth between LA and Minnesota. Then we
would talk on the phone, and he would play stuff for me over the
line. I loved working that way."

"He does smell good! I'm really aware of people's smells. I love
fragrances and perfumes. Ever since I've known Prince I've
attached a smell to him, which is lavender, and I don't know why.
He reeks of it. And I'm sure he would probably disagree with me.
He's very private, you know, and very shy. He's great when you
get to know him. Charming and funny in his own way. More than
anything, he really comes alive when he is working."

ALBUMS
'MADONNA'
(THE FIRST ALBUM)

"The songs were pretty weak and I went to England during the recording so I wasn't around . . . I wasn't in control."

"I didn't realise how crucial it was for me to break out of the disco mould before I'd nearly finished the (first) album, I wish I could have got a little more variety in there."

'LIKE A VIRGIN'

"I was surprised with how people reacted to 'Like A Virgin' because when I did the song, to me, I was singing about how something made me feel a certain way – brand-new and fresh – and everyone else interpreted it as 'I don't want to be a virgin any more. Fuck my brains out!' That's not what I sang at all."

"When I say virgin, like in my song, I'm not thinking about sexual virgin. I mean newness."

"'Like A Virgin' is a much harder album, much more aggressive than the first record. The songs on that were pretty weak. On this one I've chosen all the songs and I want them all to be hits – no fillers. That's why I've done outside songs as well as six of my own . . . I wanted every song to be strong."

'TRUE BLUE'

"She was very much in love. It was obvious . . . if she's in love she'll write love songs. If she's not in love she definitely won't be writing love songs. That's why the long songs we recorded aren't on the LP – she didn't feel that they were real enough for her at the time." Co-writer Steve Bray.

'LIKE A PRAYER'

"In other songs I've been dealing with more specific issues that mean a lot to me. They're about an assimilation of experiences I've had in my life and in relationships. They're about my mother, my father and bonds with my family about the pain of dying, or growing up and letting go."

stage

"It's so hot up here my hair-do's all fucked up.
But I'm still gonna dance my ass off for you."

STAGE

"I have my moment of exhaustion . . . but I can go for nights without sleeping if I'm not working on anything specifically. But if I'm doing a tour or working on a film I really have to be on the ball so I make sure I get to bed early. I need at least six hours sleep so I have to cut down on my social life if I want to feel good the next day. When I occasionally get eight hours sleep I find it hard to believe."

"I've been upset but I would always go on stage. I like to try to fix it first, though. I've had fights with people right before I've gone on stage, and then I've gone on stage with tears in my eyes. I would always go on stage unless something truly horrible happened."

"I swore after my last tour that I wasn't going to do another. That whole living out of a suitcase business – I don't know how Bruce Springsteen does it. I could never go on tour for a year. I told my manager that the only way I would do the tour is if I could make it interesting for myself. Because that was the challenge: being able to make a show interesting in a stadium, where you're not supposed to be interesting, where it's just this big mega-show, real impersonal. I wanted to make it really personal, even though people would be sitting really far away from me. And I think that's what we've managed to do."

"I see (her own image on the screen above the stage) and I say, 'Oh God. What have I done? What have I created? Is that me, or is that me, this small person standing here on the stage?' That's why I call the tour 'Who's That Girl': because I play a lot of characters, and every time I do a video or a song, people go, 'Oh, that's what she's like.' And I'm not like any of them. I'm all of them. I'm none of them. You know what I mean?"

"I love being on stage and I love the expressions in people's eyes and the ecstasy and the thrill but I have to have a bodyguard now for security reasons. I feel caged in hotel rooms wherever I go. In New Orleans once I took a cab to Bourbon Street. I put on a hat and pulled it down low but as soon as I stepped on to the kerb someone said 'There's Madonna.' It hasn't quite got to the point where I never go out yet. I still go running or shopping. I don't sit around contemplating my fame or how popular I am. What interests me is my confrontations with people every day and my performances at night. I don't sit and think about my record sales or how much money I have."

"After the 'Who's That Girl' tour I said to myself that I didn't want to hear any of my songs again and I didn't know whether I'd ever write another one. I returned feeling so burned out and I was convinced I wouldn't go near music for quite a while. But Pat Leonard built this new studio and I went to see it. Within an hour we'd written this great song. It amazed me."

"I am completely uninhibited on stage with 30,000 people in the audience, and I say things and dance and sing because I feel confident about it because I know what I'm doing."

ON APPEARING IN 'SPEED THE PLOUGH'

"I hated to love it and I loved to hate it. It was just gruelling, having to do the same thing every night, playing a character who is so unlike me. I didn't have a glamorous or flamboyant part; I was a scapegoat. That's one of the things that attracted me to it. Still, night after night, that character failed in the context of the play. To continue to fail each night and to walk off that stage crying, with my heart wrenched . . . it just got to me after a while. I was becoming as miserable as the character I played. So when I did *The David Letterman Show*, it was very much towards the end of the run, and I was really marking off days on the calendar."

movies

"Music was still very important to me, but I always had a great interest in films, and the thought that I could only make records for the rest of my life filled me with horror."

SCREEN SCRIBBLES

"Rock video and film aren't that different, but the public's perception of it is different. To them, the roles they've seen me do in videos are me. To me, they're characters that part of me is in. After I did *Desperately Seeking Susan*, people went 'Oh, she's really playing herself,' and I thought: 'That means I have to play an opposite character to convince everyone.' Which is a trap."

"I loved the script of (Mary Lambert's) *Siesta*, but I couldn't deal with all the nudity in it. I'm at a stage in my career where any kind of nudity would be an incredible distraction within a given movie. As far as other movies go, it's very hit-and-miss when nudity works. For instance, I loved *Betty Blue* and felt the nudity was very natural and important to the telling of the story. On the other hand, I was disturbed by the nudity in *Blue Velvet* and felt it was done for the sake of shocking the audience."

"Acting is frustrating for me, I've got to keep my energy for the three-second scenes . . . I've lost my cool a few times."

"I think it's really difficult for Americans to express passion and desire in movies. Something bad always has to happen – violence – or the relationship doesn't last. I will not be attracted to making violent films. I'm attracted to roles where women are strong, and aren't victimised. Everything I do has to be some kind of celebration of life."

"I had several meetings with Robert Stigwood, and in China I read tons of literature on *Evita*, but Stigwood really insisted on doing an operetta kind of thing, and the only way that doing *Evita* would be interesting to me is as a drama, so it didn't work. I'd love to do a movie someday where I sing, but it's hard to make a transition if I do movies about singers."

"I really want to be recognised as an actress. I've learned that if you surround yourself with great writers and great actors and a great director and a great costumier or whatever, it's pretty hard to go wrong. In the past I've been in a really big hurry to make movies and I haven't kind of taken the time to make sure all of those elements were in line and good enough. It's a waste of time to do something mediocre. Unless you absolutely believe in every aspect of it then you shouldn't waste your time."

"It takes longer to make a movie than it does to make an album, therefore I find that even if I make maybe one, or even two movies

a year, I still have several months left to make more records than
I make movies."

"I'd like to play the girl who made Alexis feel like a fool."

"Ultimately I want to direct films."

"I would rather own an art gallery than a movie studio.
Or a museum. I would rather be Peggy Guggenheim than
Harry Cohn."

"There's a little bit of you in every character that you do. I think I
had something in common with Susan in *Desperately Seeking Susan*
and I think I have a lot in common with Nikki Finn in *Who's That
Girl*, but it's not me. Still, I wouldn't have been attracted to her if
we didn't have something in common."

"I do in a way feel it would have been great in the old days (of
Hollywood). The studio system really nurtured and cared for you
in a way it doesn't now. On the other hand, your life was not your

own. Now you have more individual freedom, but you don't have anyone looking after your career in the way they did then."

"I think in the back of my mind, no matter what I was learning to do, I've always had the deepest desire to pursue acting as a career. I guess I'm sort of getting to it in a roundabout way."

HOLLYWOOD HERO?

"Oh, Jimmy Stewart! I love him so much. I would die to meet him! I can think of two incredibly favourite moments in his films that just melt me. In *It's A Wonderful Life*, there's that scene where he's standing with Donna Reed, who's talking on the phone, and he's telling her he doesn't love her as he's kissing her, and he's crying. Clearly he loves her so much. Oooooh! And then the other moment is in *Rear Window* when he gives Grace Kelly this look. She's spending the night with him, and he turns and rests his chin on the back of a chair and looks at her so lovingly. I can't describe it, but that is the way I want someone to look at me when he loves me. It's the most pure look of love and adoration. Like surrender. It's devastating."

"I'd like to work with Bob Fosse, Martin Scorcese and Jamie Foley. I love Coppola, I think he's great. Also Roman Polanski and Mike Nichols. I would have loved to make a movie with Fassbender . . . he would have been great to work with."

THE FILMS DESPERATELY SEEKING SUSAN

"Susan and I have the same sense of adventure and playfulness and flirtatiousness. She also wears a lot of my jewellery!"

"Yes, I'm Sue. Wild, free-spirited and adventurous and everybody is desperately seeking me."

"When I read the script I felt immediately that I could play the part."

"It was a real drag! There was so much sitting around, it drove me crazy . . . but it's what I'd always wanted to do."

"I had a few scenes where I was really shitting bricks! A few times I was so nervous I opened my mouth and nothing came out. I think I surprised everybody though by being one of the calmest people on the set because I was in total wonderment, just soaking everything up."

"Oh, I shared a lot with Susan. She's also an incredibly resourceful girl. She's one of those people who you don't know how she manages to look so good with so few pieces of clothing. But I have a focus and a direction. I don't think she has any of those qualities. I'm a disciplined person and I've got goals."

"When *Desperately Seeking Susan* opened in Hollywood, on the first night I definitely felt like a little girl. All the cameras, the flashes, the crowd, that applause . . . it was just great."

SHANGHAI SURPRISE

"*Shanghai Surprise* was edited as an adventure movie. They cut all my major scenes down to nothing which made me look like an airhead girl, without a character."

"I actually liked the script. Then we got there and the director (Jim Goddard) just had no knowledge of what he was doing, and it was downhill from the second day. But it was as different as I could get from *Desperately Seeking Susan*, and a truly miserable experience I learned a lot from and don't regret!"

"I didn't have a very happy time in England during the filming of *Shanghai Surprise* at Elstree. The press here were unbelievably vicious and rude. I like England but it isn't what I'm used to. In New York people are loud and say what they want. English people are far more reserved. If I go into a grocer's store here and I'm loud and I laugh at something, everybody stares. On the tubes nobody speaks much or smiles. In New York they assault you with noise."

"I think he (George Harrison) has give me more advice on how to deal with the press than how to work on the movie."

"When we were filming in England it was like the third world war. Sean and I seem to make good press. It's probably because of his reputation of being easily provoked."

"There were big rats underneath our trailers . . . I kept saying, 'I can't wait till I can look back on this thing, I can't wait.' It was a survival test. I know I can get through anything now."

"I'm extremely disappointed with it (*Shanghai Surprise*). The director didn't have an eye for the big screen and it seemed as if he was in a bit over his head. The film company wanted an action film like *Raiders Of The Lost Ark* but the script was actually a potential love story. Unfortunately it was edited as an adventure movie and they left out all the stuff that was its saving grace. We wanted it to be an old romantic movie like *African Queen* and that's what we envisioned when we read the script."

"Sean Penn asked me never to see *Shanghai Surprise*. He said, 'As a friend, don't watch it.' So I never will."
Chrissie Hynde

WHO'S THAT GIRL

"The thing I had planned doing right after *Shanghai Surprise* was *Blind Date*, over at Tri-Star. I was supposed to have approval of the leading man and the director, and they didn't tell me they'd already hired Bruce Willis. That . . . just didn't work out. But I was really excited about doing a real physical, screwball comedy, so when Jamie brought up this, it was like my reward."

"All Warner's executives were real positive about the project. It was a process – with the writers – of honing the script, making it better."

"The film *Who's That Girl* did really well in Europe where it got great reviews. I think it did badly in America because I upstaged it with my 'Who's That Girl' world tour. People were confused about the connection between the record, the tour and the movie because they all had the same title. I also think there are people who don't want me to do well in both fields."

DICK TRACY

"Breathless Moloney's a nightclub singer and she falls in love with Dick Tracy in spite of herself. I don't think she is inherently evil but she's quite accomplished in villainy. She's basically a good person."

video

"I love performing but it is very taxing to go on the
road and travel in a bus. Video has made it possible
to reach the masses without touring."

'LIKE A VIRGIN'

"We wanted me to be the modern-day worldly-wise girl that I am. But then we wanted to go back in time and use an ancient virgin."

"The lion didn't do anything he was supposed to do, and I ended up leaning against this pillar with his head in my crotch . . . I thought he was going to take a bite out of me so I lifted the veil I was wearing and had a stare-down with him and he opened his mouth and let out this huge roar. I got so frightened my heart fell in my shoe. When he finally walked away the director yelled 'Cut' and I had to take a long breather. But I could really relate to the lion. I feel like in a past life I was a lion or a cat or something."

'EXPRESS YOURSELF'

"This one I've had the most amount of input. I oversaw everything – the building of the sets, everyone's costume, I had meetings with make-up and hair and the cinematographer . . . everybody. Casting, finding the right cat – just every aspect. Kind of like making a little movie. We basically sat down and just threw out every idea we could possible conceive of and of all the things we wanted. All the imagery we wanted . . . and I had a few set ideas, for instance the cat and the idea of *Metropolis* (a 1926 German futuristic fantasy film). I definitely wanted to have that influence, that look on all the men – the workers, diligently, methodically working away.

"It was David (the director)'s idea for the cat to like lick the milk and then pour it over . . . it's great but believe me I fought him on that. I didn't want to do it. I thought it's just so over the top and silly and kind of clichéd, an art student or a film student's kind of trick. I'm glad that I gave in to him."

"The ultimate thing behind the song is that if you don't express yourself, if you don't say what you want, then you're not going to get it. And in effect you are chained down by your inability to say what you feel or go after what you want."

'LIKE A PRAYER'

"People who are really passionate and who really have an open mind, if they really watch closely I think that the video has a very positive message and that they wouldn't find fault with it. The passion . . . there's something almost sexual about it really, if you want to get really psycho-analytical about it. The video was very. . . I think it had a very positive message. It was about overcoming racism and overcoming the fear of telling the truth. So many people witness crimes and they're afraid to get involved because it'll only bring them trouble. They're afraid to stand out on a limb and stand up for someone else – I think it had a lot of positive messages.

"I mean, it's a very taboo subject to have an interracial relationship and the idea of that kind of joyousness in church. It dealt with a lot of taboos and it made people afraid. I think the people who reacted negatively to it were afraid of their own feelings that they have about those issues."

"She's always willing to deal with whatever reaction people have. Obviously if you're on a hill dancing with half a dozen burning crosses behind you, someone's going to say something."
Pat Leonard, co-songwriter of 'Like A Prayer'.

m e

"They thought they would wake up one day and I'd go away. But I'm not going to go away."

TOUGHING IT OUT

"I won't be happy until I'm as famous as God. I'm tough, ambitious, and I know exactly what I want. If that makes me a bitch – okay."

"In the beginning they thought that I was the flavour of the month, a one-act disco dolly who was just going to pop in and pop out. But slowly as the years go by I've been showing a little bit more of myself: one facet and then another."

"I've always been good at manipulating people and getting my way with charm."

"It's more than ego. It's an overwhelming interior light that I let shine without control. I am guarded by my instinct . . . it's both my faith and conscience."

"I hate polite conversation. I hate it when people stand around and go, 'Hi, how are you?' I hate words that don't have any reason or meaning. Also I hate it when people smoke in elevators and closed in places. It's just so rude."

"I've been called a tramp and a harlot and the kind of girl who would always end up in the back seat of a car."

"I know the aspect of my personality, being the vixen, the heartbreaker and the incredibly provocative girl is a very marketable image – but it's not insincere. You just can't take it seriously."

"I have to listen to the criticism that I get when it's dealing with my work. It's beneficial, I guess I don't take criticism very well but it's getting better. If I do something and there's 100 people in the room and 99 people say they liked it, I only remember the person who didn't like it."

"They used to say that I was a slut, a pig, an easy lay, a sex bomb, Minnie Mouse or even Marlene Dietrich's daughter, but I'd rather say that I'm just a hyperactive adult."

"The maid comes three days a week and on the days she doesn't I make my own bed. I've even been known to wash my own clothes."

"In everyday life I am quiet and reserved, not the housekeeper type but cool and relaxed. I don't get up in the morning wearing false eyelashes and I don't wear fancy underwear when I'm cooking popcorn. I am a nice little ducky."

"No matter what I do, there will always be people who think of me as a little disco tart."

"I bought Olivia Newton John's house in Malibu, California, and an apartment in New York because I couldn't live in hotels any longer."

"I laugh at myself. I don't take myself completely seriously. I think that's another quality that people have to hold on to . . . you *have* to laugh, especially at yourself. I do it in most of the things I do, and most of the videos that I make and most of my performances. Even in my concerts there were so many moments when I just stood still and laughed at myself."

"It's healthy for me to force myself to move about independently. It helps me touch base with reality. I could never live a sheltered life . . . that would drive me insane."

FAULTS

"Impatience. I just can't stand waiting. I always want everything right away. Nothing came as fast as I wanted it."

"I have mixed emotions about the way I look. I wish I was taller. I probably look taller 'cause I've got such a big mouth. I think it's important to try and look larger than life if you're a performer."

"Oh . . . I can be a bitch. Deep down inside I'm really a nice girl. But, certainly, I can be a bitch. I'm a perfectionist, and I'm under lots of pressure. Sometimes you have to be a bitch to get things done."

"I think I stand for a whole lot of things in fans' minds, a lot of kinds of stereotypes, like the whole sex-goddess image and the blonde thing. But mainly I think they feel that most of my music is really positive, and I think they appreciate that, particularly the women. I think I stand for everything they're really taught *not* to do, so maybe I provide them with a little bit of encouragement."

"I am ambitious. But if I weren't as talented as I am ambitious I would be a gross monstrosity. I am not surprised by my success because it feels natural."

"I'm a terrible cook. I just wait for someone to take me out to dinner. I like Japanese and French food."

"I'm very indecisive: yes – no – yes. In my career I make pretty good decisions, but in my personal life I cause constant havoc by changing my mind every five minutes."

STYLE

"An image and a good hook can get you in the room, but something has to keep you in the room."

"I used to be such an outgoing crazy lass. I went out of my way to make statements with my clothing and I brazenly looked people in the eye when I walked down the streets and rode the subway."

"I think I have an original sense of style, and I think that people are unconsciously copying my style. My style is a combination of a lot of things and maybe theirs is too. Either it's coincidence or they're copying my style – it's just obvious. But sometimes, when you see people do that, it's really cute, you know? But sometimes it isn't."

"I act out of instinct, just like an animal. Suddenly I couldn't stand all that hair of mine and all those baubles any more. That image had to be cleaned thoroughly. My new look is innocent, straightforward and feminine. I feel perfectly at home in this new skin."

"I live in a huge loft – 2,000 square feet – in Soho in Lower Manhattan. It's where all the artists are. Talking Head's David Byrne is my neighbour. My loft space has bare floors, windows

on every wall, a bed, a table and chairs. That's it. Oh no . . . I have
lots of mirrors for my choreography.''

"New York's very street, busier than London. I eat in Little Italy
and always have spudini, an appetiser. It's different cheeses fried
in olive oil served on a kind of pizza base . . . mmm. It's delicious
and fattening.''

"My image is a natural extension of my performance so my songs
may not be deliberately sexual but the way I achieve them could be.''

"With the crucifixes I was exorcising the extremes that my
upbringing dwelt on. Putting them up on the wall and throwing
darts at them. And the BOY TOY thing was a joke, a tag name
given to me when I first arrived in New York because I flirted
with the boys. All the graffiti artists wore their nicknames on their
belt buckles.''

"I like clothes you can move about in – I don't like it when
someone looks as if they're glued into their outfit.''

"Exercise is absolutely necessary for me because I don't dance
any more.''

"I like having a supple body. It allows you to move more easily,
and it's also visually more appealing.''

"Basques are restricting. They have ribs that make you feel
you're suffocating.''

"I figured if I'm gonna present myself as a virgin on TV, I should
do it for you.''
(To Johnny Carson, 1987.)

"Bruce Springsteen was born to run. I was born to flirt.''

SEX, DRUGS AND
ROCK 'N' ROLL

"I liked my body when I was growing up and I wasn't ashamed of it.
I liked boys and didn't feel inhibited by them. Maybe it comes from
having brothers and sharing a bathroom. The boys got the wrong
impression of me at high school. They mistook forwardness for
promiscuity. When they don't get what they want, they turn on
you. I went through a period when all the girls thought I was loose
and the boys said I was a nymphomaniac. The first boy I ever slept
with was my boyfriend and we'd been going out a long time.''

"When I turned 17 I moved to New York because my father wouldn't let me date boys at home. I never saw a naked body when I was a kid – gosh, when I was 17 I still hadn't seen a penis."

"I'm sexy. How can I avoid it? That's the essence of me. I would have to put a bag over my head and body but then my voice would come across. And *it's* sexy."

"Even after I made love for the first time, I still felt I was a virgin. I didn't lose my virginity until I knew what I was doing."

"Losing my virginity? I thought of it as a career move."

"I wouldn't like to sleep with a guy who was a virgin. I'd have to teach him stuff and I don't have the patience."

"I think my voice sounds innocent and sexual at the same time. That's what I tell people anyway, but they look at me and go, 'Innocent, huh?'"

"Sex symbol? I guess I would be perceived as that, because I have a typically voluptuous body and I express sexual desire without really caring what people think about me."

"Books are my next favourite thing . . . after kissing my husband."

"I don't take drugs: I never did. All the feelings that drugs are supposed to produce in you – confidence or energy – I can produce naturally. The only problem is going to sleep. But I never take pills . . . I drink herbal teas."

"I can go for nights without sleeping if I'm not working on anything specifically, but if I'm doing a tour or working on a film I really have to be on the ball so I make sure I get to bed early. I need at least six hours sleep so I have to cut down on my social life if I want to feel good the next day. When I occasionally get eight hours sleep I find it hard to believe."

"I work at not being self-destructive."

FASHION

"The thing is, I wouldn't even be blonde now except that I'm doing *Dick Tracy* and I had to dye my hair blonde. It took me so long to grow my hair out and I really wanted to have dark hair. I felt kind of great having my own hair colour for the first time in years. Women with blonde hair are perceived as much more sexual

and much more impulsive . . . fun-loving but not as layered, not as deep, not serious."

"Being blonde is definitely a different state of mind. I can't really put my finger on it, but the artifice of being blonde has some incredible sort of sexual connotation. Men really respond to it. I love blonde hair but it really does something different to you. I feel more grounded when I have dark hair, and I feel more ethereal when I have light hair. It's unexplainable. I also feel more Italian when my hair is dark."

"I'd like to see every teenage girl in America dressed up like me."

"I'm proud of my trashy image – my clothes come from the street."

"I think I always make the worst dressed list. It's just silly. But it is kind of nice having something you can always count on."

"I've changed my image. If you spend a couple of years wearing lots of layers of clothes and tons of jewellery, it takes you forever to get dressed. And if your hair is long and crazy, you just get the urge to take it all off, strip yourself down and cut your hair just for relief. Everybody does that, you know."

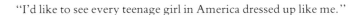

PAST, PRESENT AND FUTURE

"When your name is Madonna it's best to become one."

"Sometimes I just assume that I'm going to live for ever."

"I'd love to be a memorable figure in the history of entertainment in some sexual comic tragic way. I'd like to leave the impression that Marilyn Monroe did, to be able to arouse so many different feelings in people."

"I would like to write a searing love story, probably semi-autobiographical, you know, because it's best to draw on your personal experiences."

WHAT'S IN A NAME?

"I never remember feeling tormented for my name. But then I went to Catholic schools. It wasn't until I came to New York that I became aware that it was such an unusual name. People just assumed it was a stage name."

"My mother is the only other person I have heard of named Madonna.

INNER THOUGHTS

When I got involved in the music industry everyone thought I took it as a stage name. So I let them think that – it's pretty glamorous."

"I worry about worrying too much, I worry too much about what other people think. I worry about hurting people and I do it a lot, though not intentionally. And I worry about living up to my own expectations. That's helped make me a very determined individual but it's also made me too much of a manic about things and too hard on myself."

"I can be arrogant sometimes, but I never mean it intentionally. I can be really snotty to people but that's not anything new really. I always acted like a star long before I was one. If people don't see my sense of humour then I come off as being expensive, but I always endear myself to people when I find their weaknesses and they acknowledge it. It's the people who try to hide everything and try to make you think they're so cool that I can't stand."

"I'm vulnerable to people who want to rape my soul. You know, like journalists. It's weird – it depends on what kind of mood you're in. Sometimes I'll be doing a photo session with someone that I've done a lot of work with, and all of a sudden I feel like they've seen too much and I don't want them to look at me any more. Usually I'm pretty outgoing and gregarious, but I can be really shy about things sometimes."

"I remember the past when I can't go to sleep."

"I've always wanted to be taller. I feel like a shrimp, but that's the way it goes. I'm five-foot four-and-a-half-inches – that's actually average. Everything about me is average. Everything's normal, in the books. It's the things inside me that make me not average."

"I've never worn a jewel in my belly button, but if I did it would be a ruby or an emerald – not a diamond."

"If a hundred belly buttons were lined up against a wall, I could definitely pick out which was mine.

"I have the most perfect belly button. When I stick my fingers in it, I feel a nerve in the centre of my body shoot up my spine.

"I think if someone becomes hugely successful the public becomes disgusted with them and begins to wish the star would slip on a banana peel. That's the basic aspect of human nature."

feminism

"I think women are intimidated by women who are incredibly ambitious or competitive because it's easier to deal with girls who aren't. It's easier to deal with people who aren't. But I never really think consciously of the fact that I'm a girl or anything like that. In fact, I think I've had advantages because I'm a girl."

FEMINISM

"People have this idea that if you're sexual and beautiful and
provocative, then there's nothing else you could possibly offer.
People have always had that image about women. And while it
might have seemed like I was behaving in a stereotypical way,

at the same time I was also masterminding it. I was in control of everything I was doing, and I think that when people realised that, it confused them. It's not like I was saying, 'Don't pay any attention to the clothes – to the lingerie – I'm wearing.' Actually, the fact that I was wearing those clothes was meant to drive home the point that you can be sexy and strong at the same time. In a way it was necessary to wear the clothes."

"I don't think about the work I do in terms of feminism. I certainly feel that I give women strength and hope, particularly young women. So in that respect, I feel my behaviour is feminist. But I'm certainly not militant about it, nor do I exactly premeditate it."

"When women didn't like me I simply chalked it up to the reason why women always have a problem with me: I think that women who are strong, or women who wanted to be strong or be respected, were taught that they had to behave like men, or not be sexy or feminine or something, and I think it pissed them off that I was doing that. Also, I think for the most part men have always been the aggressors sexually. Through time immemorial they've always been in control. So I think sex is equated with power in a way, and that's scary. It's scary for men that women should have that power – or to have that power and be sexy at the same time."

"Plenty of people are getting my message. I'm not going to change the world in a day. I don't know . . . maybe it never will be where men and women are equal. They're too different. I mean . . . it just seems that as long as women are the ones that give birth to children, it'll never really change. I'm not saying that in a sad way. I think more and more women will be able to have more freedom to do whatever they want, and they won't have so many prejudices thrown at them, but I think it would be much too idealistic to say that one day we will never be discriminated against because we're women."

"People say I've set back the women's movement 30 years – but I think that women weren't ashamed of their bodies in the fifties. They luxuriated in their femininity and believed whole-heartedly in it. Women aren't like men. They can do things that men can't, mentally and physically. If people don't get the humour in my act, then they don't want to get it."

religion

"If I was to change my name, I'd use my
confirmation name Veronica. I chose her because
she wiped the face of Jesus, which I thought was
really romantic."

MADONNA
ON RELIGION

"I don't go to church but I believe in God. When I was little
I had all the usual feelings of guilt. I was very conscious of God
watching everything I did. Until I was 12 I believed the devil was
in the basement and I would run up the stairs fast so he wouldn't
grab my ankles. I've always carried around a few rosaries. There
was a turquoise coloured one my grandmother gave me a long
time ago which I wore as a necklace. It isn't sacrilegious to me.
I thought the huge crucifixes nuns wore with their habits were
beautiful."

"I loved nuns when I was growing up. I thought they were
beautiful. For several years I wanted to be a nun. I saw them as
really pure, disciplined, above average people. They had these
serene faces. Nuns are sexy."

"I had my own ideas about God and then I had the ideas that
I thought were imposed on me. I believe in God. I believe that
everything that you do comes back to you, I believe in the innate
goodness of people and the importance of that."

"When I was growing up I was religious in a passionate adolescent
way. Jesus Christ was like a movie star, my favourite idol of all."

"Crucifixes are sexy because there's a naked man on them."

"Once we got older and we could drive ourselves my father . . . um my parents (her father and stepmother) . . . would go to the earlier Mass and we'd say we were going to go to the later one. We'd all get in the car together and we'd go down to the doughnut shop and then we'd go to the church and pick up a flyer (leaflet) like we'd been there, you know, and we'd make up something that the priest said during the sermon . . . I think my father knew all along that we were lying . . ."

"I don't make fun of Catholicism. I deeply respect Catholicism – its mystery and fear and oppressiveness, its passion and its discipline and its obsession with guilt."

"I don't think a song like 'Act Of Contrition' is intended to offend anyone, just to be fun. But I think I would be offended – I was raised by a Catholic family, and the design of the world is made to offend the Christian religion. You're talking about 30 years of Christian guilt and certain things go through you."

"I pray when I'm in trouble or when I'm happy. When I feel any sort of extreme. I pray when I feel so great that I think I need to check in with myself and recognise how good life is. I know that sounds silly, but when it seems there's so much bullshit around, it's important just to remind myself of the things I have to be grateful for. On the other hand, when I'm feeling really bad or sad, I pray to try to reassure myself. It's all a kind of rationalisation. I can't describe the way I pray. It has nothing to do with religion."

"Once you're a Catholic, you're always a Catholic – in terms of your feelings of guilt and remorse and whether you've sinned or not. Sometimes I'm wracked with guilt when I needn't be, and that, to me, is left over from my Catholic upbringing. Because in Catholicism you are a born sinner and you are a sinner all your life. No matter how you try to get away with it, the sin is within you all the time."

"Catholicism is not a soothing religion. It's a painful religion. We're all gluttons for punishment."

"My favourite crucifix is real big and chunky . . . actually it's a piece of art, but I can't wear it on stage 'cause it's so heavy it might swing up and hit me on the head."

caring

"While Aids is a big problem it's important not to forget the rain forests. Every minute a plot of land the size of a baseball pitch disappears."

 CARING

"There's a lot of terrible things happening in the world today and there's a lot of people that need our help and there's a lot of environmental issues that need to be dealt with. In terms of Aids I just know so many people who have died of Aids and it's such a serious problem. Like, so much of the arts community in New York. I feel like in five years from now all of my friends will be dead. It really hits home with me. It's a very serious matter."

"Remember what you see may not be what you get. Avoid casual sex and you'll avoid Aids. And stay away from people who shoot drugs too." Madonna's advert for an Aids campaign.

"I'm not going to change the world in a day."

"Peace, man. Make love, not war. That's all."

"And then the Brazilian rain forest – I didn't think that it was such a big deal until I got all the facts about it. It really is, more than the threat of a nuclear war, which may or may not happen. If we destroy the rain forest we are destroying ourselves, and it's

happening right now. In 50 years the entire rain forest will be
gone. We need the rain forest for oxygen, we need the rain forest
to absorb the carbon dioxide that goes into the atmosphere from
all the cars and all the pollution and we need the forests to help
find cures for Aids and cancer (because many medical cures are
developed from plants and animals). There are believed to be
many many undiscovered species in the rain forest that may
become extinct without us ever knowing about them which is
an important issue for me. My mum died of cancer and my best
friend died of Aids (Martin Burgoyne, designer of the American
sleeve for 'Lucky Star'). It's a really vital important issue."

the things they say

about
madonna

"I think a lot of people feel exploited by Madonna, but then again everyone's got so many expectations about a relationship with her. She's very intense immediately with somebody, very friendly. Then, if there is any cooling of that, it's taken to be rejection."

Dan Gilroy, Former Boyfriend.

"If people feel exploited by Madonna – that's resentment of someone who's got drive. It seems like you're leaving people behind or you're stepping on them, and the fact is you're moving and they're not . . . Madonna doesn't care if she ruffles someone's feathers."
Steve Bray, former boyfriend.

"Madonna manipulates in her own way but I don't think there's a mean bone in her body . . . maybe a knuckle or two."
Mark Kamins, former boyfriend.

"I think we were in 'like' rather than in 'love'. It was a good fun time, guaranteed a laugh a day – Madonna has a great sense of humour. She's now what I consider an icon of the eighties and, yes, we're still good friends."
DJ John 'Jellybean' Benitez, former boyfriend.

"I made her cry. I screamed at her and told her she was a manipulative egomaniac who didn't give a damn about anyone. She once provoked me to such a state of anger that I bashed my fists through the door and broke my wrist."
Camille Barbone, former agent/manager.

"I just said no. At that point 'Like A Virgin' was out and I wasn't interested. A girl rolling around on the floor? I'm not really into that sort of thing."
Co-writer Pat Leonard.

"She's the kind of person that really does get up at five in the morning to go swimming. She wasn't at all prima donna-ish.

She wasn't one of those people that want to be alone and sit in their trailer the whole time. I think she has much more of a sense of humour than people give her credit for. Too many people take that femme fatale stuff at face value."
Film director Susan Seidelman.

"Madonna simply looks like an over-made-up little broad. All this posturing . . . if Madonna is the scourge of young womanhood, then young womanhood is sillier than I thought."
Agony aunt Anna Raeburn.

"My first impression on meeting Madonna? I thought she had a lot of style. And she crossed over a lot of boundaries 'cos everyone in the rock clubs played her, the black clubs, the gay, the straight . . . and very few records have that appeal.

"Was she confident in the studio? Not on the records I produced. She wasn't involved in the production. She was still learning 'What does this do?' But she was very inquisitive.

"She took advantage of the opportunities given to her, other people do the same thing."
Remix master John 'Jellybean' Benitez.

"I like Madonna having a beauty spot in a different place on every photograph. I love it. I've started doing it too. I've got one by my nipple right now."
Wayne Hussey, The Mission.

"You know, Madonna goes through about five or six costume changes . . . we go through two. It can be a real panic to get your clothes on and off in time, especially if it's hot – the clothes stick to you, the buttons have a tendency not to come undone . . ."
David Williams, one of Madonna's guitarists.

"I find it ridiculous when people accuse Madonna of selling sex. Sex and rock 'n' roll fit together so perfectly that everyone in this business sells sex. Boy George, The Beatles, Elvis Presley, Van Halen, Prince – who isn't selling sex? Maybe Barry Manilow, but that's only because he's after an older market, so he sells love. Madonna isn't pushing sex anything like she could if she really wanted to. Her look is a hot 'I'm 100 per cent woman' look, and I think that's great. Rock is full of boys who look like girls and girls who look like boys. Madonna doesn't have to put on black leather and kick the shit out of a motor cycle gang to be cool. I don't

understand why people find a girl looking like a girl to be at all
offensive. She's not a stripper type, so what's the problem?"
Michael Rosenblatt, former Sire executive.

"She's able to do something our parents would never let us get
away with – that whole slut image. It's usually just the guys who
get to do that."
16-year-old fan.

"I met her once in a club in London when she was just starting up
and she was really sweet – I said 'Hello Madonna, you are
wonderful'. . . I thought 'Yeah! She's just like me! This is the kind
of girl I could get together with . . .'"
Mark Moore of S'Express.

"I'd probably get along with her. I'm a strong person like she is
and we'd probably have a lot to talk about."
Debbie Gibson.

"Madonna studied dance at college and had great rhythm.
Drumming came naturally to her so we gave her the job. One
night she decided she wanted to have a go at singing so we let her
do a number at one of our gigs, and that was it. She was hooked.
At the time we had two singers in the band already and didn't need
another one so she quit. Probably one of the best moves she's
ever made."
Ed and Dan Gilroy of The Breakfast Club.

"I remember the very first time I met her at this party, she was
wearing a kind of circus outfit . . . very short with a tutu and
leggings a darker shade of blue than her tutu. *Sure* she had
incredible style. Absolutely. And she had olive oil in her hair
which made it quite strange and matted and those were the kinds
of things people were doing then. It was definitely influenced by
punk but you could see she was moving in her own direction.
It was quite weird really at the party, because she was just kind
of sitting there and she seemed kind of depressed or something –
I think she'd come to the party with someone she didn't want to
be with. So I was her dancing partner."
Dan Gilroy.

"She was an exceptional dancer. Many dancers can kick and
exhibit acrobatic body control, but that is just run of the mill,
taken for granted. Madonna had the power, the intensity to go
beyond mere physical performance into something far more
exciting. That intensity is the first thing I look for in a dancer, and
Madonna had it. It was sad that she left dance, but I knew she had
the power, that she would succeed at whatever she tried. Madonna
simply has the magical quality that a great artist needs."
Dance instructor Pearl Lang.

"In many respects she's the perfect pop artist."
George Michael.

"In a very sophisticated way her music and image characterises
that essential dumbness that appeals to just about everybody."
Mick Jagger.

"She is an ideal icon, her skilful stage act, image and music combining to make an oddly innocent pop phenomenon, harking back to the flirtatious glamour of earlier times: it was an illusion then, more so now; but she seems likely to endure one way or another."
Penguin Encyclopedia Of Popular Music.

"Madonna reinforces everything absurd and offensive. Desperate womanhood. Madonna is closer to organised prostitution than anything else."
Morrissey.

"I see her at gym quite often – we talk about which aerobics teachers are best. I think I have hyper-gymnasium but she works out much more than I do. She's heavy duty."
Belinda Carlisle.

"I think she looked better with a chest ."
Patsy Kensit.

"I think she's really great. I respect and admire her and think she's really talented."
Susanna Hoffs of The Bangles.

"She looks like the bleedin' Hulk with a wig on."
Phil Oakey of The Human League.

"She looks like she stinks."
Robert Smith of The Cure.

"I think she's really beautiful. I don't think she can sing, though."
Ali Campbell of UB40.

"She's fantastic, one of my favourite people in the world. She's a really incredible artist, she really knows what she wants."
Nile Rodgers, producer of 'Like A Virgin'.

"My experience working with Madonna was so valuable. I learned so much."
Michael Kamins, the DJ who first played Madonna's tapes at the Danceteria disco and ex-boyfriend.

"Comparing Madonna with Marilyn Monroe is like comparing Raquel Welch with the back of a bus!"
Boy George.

"Madonna acts like a porn queen on heat."
Leading American churchwoman Margaret Scott.

"To have someone with good manners is more important than
having a good actress."
**Tim Rice on the auditioning of Madonna to play the part of
Eva Peron in the film version of *Evita*.**

"That woman has more sensuality in her ear than most women
have got anywhere in their bodies."
Stephen Jon Lewick, director of *A Certain Sacrifice*.

"I was in hospital when I heard about Madonna. From what
I heard I wanted to sign her immediately. You know you don't
care normally what you look like when you're in hospital. But
I shaved, I combed my hair and I got a new dressing gown.
From what I'd heard I was excited to meet Madonna."
Sire Records boss, Seymour Stein.

"It hit me right away. I could tell she had the drive to match
her talent."
Stein after that first meeting.

"Madonna slows down this plow. Her ineptitude is scandalously
thorough. She moves as if she were operated by remote control
several cities away."
CBS TV critic on Madonna's role in *Speed The Plow*.

"It's a relief to report that this rock star's performance is safely
moved from her Hollywood persona. Madonna serves
Mr Mamet's play much as she did the Susan Seidelman film
Desperately Seeking Susan with intelligent, scrupulously disciplined
comic acting.
***New York Times* theatre critic on *Speed The Plow*.**

"She's just a flavour of the month."
Lyricist Tim Rice.

"She's so strong, beautiful and manipulative. All of which means
she writes great songs."
Kim of Sonic Youth.

the things madonna says

about them!

George Harrison

"I wasn't a Beatlemaniac. I think I didn't really appreciate their songs till I was much older. But he's a great boss. Very understanding and sympathetic."

Elvis Presley

"It would be fitting to say he died on my birthday but I don't believe he did. The supposed date of death is the day I was born, August 16, but I reckon the King lives, I think he's in Michigan which means there is a room for me at Graceland."

Billy Idol

"I was considering doing a song with Billy Idol. That would have been good because we're both white and plastic and blonde."

Prince

"Why aren't (critics) letting (sexuality) stand in the way of appreciating Prince's music? He was certainly just as sexually provocative, if not more than I was. I wasn't talking about giving head. He was much more specific than I was."

"I think Prince lives a very isolated life and I don't, and that is the big difference between us. And I just try to be a positive influence on him. I've always been a fan. I think that he's incredible. He's very courageous and he causes lots of controversy too which is great . . . and I think he is a brilliant musician. We've gotten together a couple of times in the hope of working with each other in some way. Originally we were going to do a musical together and we were going to write the music for it – that didn't really pan out. We just kept getting together. He seemed to fight the idea of just writing songs for a record together because he's done that with so many people."

"He came to see me in the play I did last summer in New York and he, just for the hell of it, put together a tape of some rough things that we'd done in all the meetings that we'd had. 'Love Song' was one of the songs and I just said 'You know, this is crazy, it's such a great song – why not put it on the record?' It seemed to relate to all the other songs because it's about a relationship that's a love/hate relationship. So he agreed to it and we kind of sent the tapes back and forth to each other and we'd keep building it. It was like he would write a sentence and I would add on to it and then send it back to him and he would continue the story, basically. It was fun. I played the keyboards myself and because I don't know that much, it kind of came out strange and interesting."

Michael Jackson

"I'd like to dance and work with Michael Jackson now I've done Prince but it'll never happen. He has a shyness towards women. He'd probably rather die than dance with me!"

"I wanted to be Michael Jackson. He electrified me and I wanted to be that way too."

"As a teenager I was a Michael Jackson wannabe. I thought to myself 'I can do everything he can do only I'm a girl'. . ."

"Last week I was invited to dinner with Michael Jackson and (producer) Quincy Jones. But these things are really kinda boring. It's more interesting to keep a low profile, not show up at everything."
May 1984.

Boy George

"He had big high heels on and a big entourage of people all dressed the same. He kept going on about this group he had, but I wouldn't believe him. Six months later he was number one."

"Boy George makes me sick."

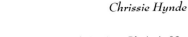

GIRLS

Tammy Wynette

"As a teenager me and my best mate used to wear our hair up like Tammy Wynette. And we wore tons of lipstick and really badly applied make up."

Chrissie Hynde

"When I first started singing Chrissie Hynde was a great inspiration. I thought she had a great voice and was gutsy . . ."

Shirley Temple

"I really wanted to dance like her, I really wanted to be the new Shirley Temple."

Nancy Sinatra

"I loved 'These Boots Are Made For Walking' and I loved her image. The go-go boots, mini-skirt, blonde hair and false eyelashes . . ."

Chaka Khan

"I'm a great fan of Chaka Khan. Her voice is absolutely incredible. I only wish I could sing like her. How did she ever manage to get that quality of tone? A true Godsend."

Debbie Harry

"I loved the fact that she was a woman in charge of what she was doing. She gave me courage."

Marilyn Monroe

"She was my first movie idol. When I saw her and Brigitte Bardot I wanted to make my hair blonde and wear pointy bras . . ."

"I liked Carole Lombard, Judy Holliday, Marilyn Monroe. They were all incredibly funny, and they were silly and sweet. I just saw myself in them, my funniness, and my need to boss people around and at the same time be taken care of. My knowingness and my innocence. Both."

"At first I enjoyed the comparisons between me and Marilyn Monroe. I saw it as a compliment; she was very sexy. Then it started to annoy me because no one wants to be continuously reminded of someone else. You want people to see that you have your own statement to make."

"I love dresses like Marilyn Monroe wore, those fifties styles really tailored to fit a voluptuous body."

"Marilyn Monroe was a victim and I'm not. That's why there's really no comparison."

"I want to be a symbol of something. That's what I think when I think of conquering. It's that you stand for something. I mean, as far as I'm concerned Marilyn Monroe conquered the world . . . she stands for something."